CW00693338

SCOTTISH DIESELS
A Colour Portfolio

David Cross

Ian Allan
PUBLISHING

Front cover: Although the picture was taken on 5 May 1979 winter snowfalls are still evident on the hills behind the important junction station of Crianlarich. Once a three-way junction, by 1979 only the lines from Glasgow to Fort William and Oban remained, the line through Glen Ogle to Dunblane having closed on 1 November 1965.

Pictured just west of Crianlarich alongside the A82 road is Class 27 No 27032 heading for Oban. The train is 1B11, the 12.55 Glasgow, Queen Street to Oban service, with the next stop at Lower Tyndrum. No 27032 had begun life as D5379 in March 1962 in North London, lasting in traffic until May 1985 before being withdrawn from Inverness depot.

Crianlarich is some 59 miles from Glasgow and remains an important railway centre with an extensive engineers' yard, an active goods yard (for timber) and an excellent and friendly refreshment room! *Les Riley*

Title page: Easing out of Crianlarich station heading south with an Oban–Glasgow Queen Street service is NBL Type 2 No D6107 with Gresley passenger brake No E162E. The date is 15 April 1968.

The locomotive was one of the first NBL Type 2s to be reliveried into Rail Blue. At first designated a Class 21 locomotive, it was one of 20 converted and refurbished to Class 29, in this case in February 1967. In active service for just 12½ years, from March 1959 to October 1971, the locomotive was stored three times covering 40 months of inactivity, so working shots are hard to find. Here just six months before final withdrawal (and disposal at nearby Glasgow works in 1972) No D6107 rumbles away from Crianlarich towards Glasgow and into history. *Derek Cross*

First published 2005

ISBN (10) 0 7110 3082 0
ISBN (13) 978 0 7110 3082 0

© David Cross 2005

Published by Ian Allan Publishing

an imprint of Ian Allan Publishing Ltd, Hersham, Surrey KT12 4RG

Printed in England by Ian Allan Printing Ltd, Hersham, Surrey KT12 4RG

0510/B1

Visit the Ian Allan Publishing website at www.ianallanpublishing.com

Foreword

I was more than a little delighted when David Cross asked me to write a few words as the foreword for the second volume of his late father Derek's photographs of diesel locomotives at work north of the border.

David and I have been friends since our careers briefly crossed in the mid-1970s. Although I had met Derek on only one brief occasion, I have always felt that our outlook on railway photography had much in common, though separated by a generation of railway operations and photographic styles.

Firstly, Derek and I both practised the art in southern Scotland. Photography north of the border can be a frustrating pastime, with long periods of indifferent weather and infrequent trains. Secondly, Derek realised early on that railways were worthy subjects for the camera after steam had finished, echoing my own views, though in my case railway photography did not become practical until well after steam's demise. Thirdly, I, like Derek, have a feeling for the railways and railwaymen of Scotland, and in particular Ayrshire. Until recently it was my job to arrange rail trips to locations like Killoch, Knockshinnoch, Waterside (now Chalmerston), Broomhills and Ayr Harbour. Although my daily dealings were with a younger generation of traincrews, I cannot look at the two previous volumes of Derek's Ayrshire photos without feeling a bond of familiarity or kinship — call it what you will — with the workings that were so familiar to Derek. The fact that when not on duty I would often attempt to record these workings on film (though considerably less successfully!) strengthened the feeling that Derek and I were engaged on the same quest.

Derek's work in the post-1968 era covered several now-extinct diesel types, like the disastrous early North British Locomotive Co diesels and 'Claytons', through to the more successful Sulzer Type 2s and English Electric Type 4s. My own experiences — and photography — have been with Classes 20, 37, 56, 60 and latterly with the now ubiquitous Class 66. Therein lies the conflict between the professional and photographer. General Motors' workhorse is common and often unspectacular for the camera, but is an operating man's dream, needing little more than fuelling regularly to keep it running on a 24/7 basis, all over Scotland.

Derek's influence on later generations of photographers is still considerable, despite the changing train styles and weather patterns.

I wonder what he would have thought of 'Sprinters' and 'Voyagers', unchecked lineside vegetation, the near death and reincarnation of the Ayrshire coal industry, the singling of parts of the Glasgow & South Western Railway main line, and the subsequent unforeseen boom in Scottish open-cast coal movement to English power stations as well as vast tonnages of coal imported through Hunterston, bound mainly for Longannet.

We must be grateful that David has made so many of his father's pictures available to all through these excellent colour albums. The fact that the famous view of the Clyde Bridge just north of Crawford on the West Coast main line is referred to by Lanarkshire-based gricers as 'Derek Cross's bridge' is a fitting if unofficial tribute. Sit back and enjoy the pictures!

Bob Avery
Carluke, Lanarkshire
March 2005

Left: The late Derek Cross in his element.

Introduction

This book is a follow-up to my earlier book *The Heyday of the Scottish Diesels* and covers diesel operations in Scotland in broad terms for the 15 years between 1967 and 1982. The book, as the title suggests, attempts to cover the whole country, taking advantage of the breathtaking scenery that the railways in Scotland provide. I have also tried to feature as many classes of locomotive as possible (in those days there was some choice!) and have been able to include some 20 different types.

The fact that 20 different classes of locomotive and multiple-unit are included highlights the fact that this 15-year period in Scottish railway history was one of change, variety and interest. During the late 1960s and early 1970s English Electric Class 50s arrived in Scotland, DMUs gave way to Class 27s and, before the end of the decade, to Class 47/7s on the vital Glasgow to Edinburgh link, while electrics appeared in 1974 which changed aspects of the West Coast

main line operations forever. And, of course, 'Rail Blue' ruled after the green livery, which had dominated the 1960s, and before the 'stripes' which dominated the 1980s.

The majority of the pictures were taken by my late father, Derek Cross, some by me and about a dozen by a family friend, Les Riley. I am very pleased that Les has released his colour material to me for this book and I hope you will enjoy this new unpublished material. Les, at the time, was employed by British Rail, travelled extensively, had a love of Scotland and had an eye for a picture along the same lines as Derek. His collection is of quality and should this book sell as well as the 'Heyday' did, we might see more of his work in future.

A number of people who bought *The Heyday of the Scottish Diesels* have commented on how Derek managed to photograph such a variety of material and how he got to some of the places where pictures were taken. Well, he was sixteen stone and

persuasive! In addition, he lived in a time when security, health and safety at work and 'jobsworths' did not feature to any degree as they do today. Relationships built during the steam era with drivers and guards, signalmen, permanent way staff and local managers all 'matured' during the 1970s as these railway staff progressed, became more senior, and allowed Derek perhaps even greater access to the railways of Scotland. For many years he had maintained excellent contacts with the very active Scottish Region PR department in Glasgow. The department also helped as it would often commission him to record pictorially something new or of interest that was happening in Scotland. An all-lines photographic permit helped as well but perhaps not as much as you might have expected, the 'train in the landscape' being his stock in trade, where fields were accessed as often as the trackside. The lack of lineside vegetation in those days also helped him very much. As steam ended, a new generation of photographers emerged who tended to include the train in almost a social context, a concept Derek never really embraced. Indeed, the odd shed shot was about as close as Derek got to this modern-age photography, which he did not much care for.

It was, however, the variety of train types and traction that sustained his interest in diesels in Scotland during the period of this book. Derek enjoyed this and the unpredictability of just what might appear in his viewfinder. In the book two specific trains are featured which completely confirm this. The Perth to Manchester empty vans and the 14.15 Edinburgh to Newcastle semi-fast service are featured five times and these five pictures feature five different types of locomotive. I also take some credit for Derek's continued interest because in the late 1970s I went abroad to work and Derek was asked to keep me up to date and communicate by colour slide! I'm sure you'll agree he did me proud.

There are probably more of my own efforts in this book than in the previous 'Heyday' book, simply because it covers a later era, broadly the 1970s. Although photographic expeditions (his words) with Derek were great fun, the advent of teenage years led to the first of David Cross's solo photographic trips — nothing too fancy, as student funds even then were hard to come by. A 10-year-old Humber Sceptre, which was not fuel efficient, a friend's Triumph Herald, where journeys in the dark were very hazardous if it was raining because you could have either the lights or the wipers but never both together, Freedom of Scotland tickets and visits to locations in Ayrshire by pushbike all contributed to augmenting Derek's collection and the photographs we see in this book. Getting bitten to death by midges whilst under canvas at Kyle of Lochalsh, feeling very ill after a stranger recommended Mackeson to me as a nice drink in Aberdeen and getting lost in a none-too-salubrious corner of Glasgow did not deter me.

I am frequently asked about Derek's cars. Well, in a word, fast, and sometimes none too polite to other road users — that's probably why people still ask and remember years later. For the late Bill Anderson and Derek, Sunbeams were their preferred choice. Bill favoured Rapiers and Derek his white Alpine until it caught fire. After that Derek had three Rover 2000s, two white and one blue, supplemented by a Land Rover for use in the winter and for off-road expeditions. I have doubts as to whether Derek would still have a licence doing the same today!

A number of people often ask about what cameras Derek used. For those of you who have read this before, because it changes very little, I apologise. Over half the images in this 'Colour Portfolio' were taken on large format transparencies of 2¼in x 3¼in rectangular negatives with just eight to a 120 size film. Later on this changed to 12 negatives of 2¼in square size to one 120 size film. The film used was almost exclusively Agfa CT18 and the hardware a Linhof press camera, which was later replaced by a Rollei SL66, of which he spoke very highly. The colour slide material was taken on Kodachrome II film with a 35mm Leica with interchangeable lenses or an early Canon SLR. Through the 1970s film speed improved a great deal and so with faster film it became easier to take colour pictures in poor weather. This was a welcome development, especially in Scotland in winter, and in recent years film speed has progressed further, allowing present day photographers to take pictures in virtually all weather conditions.

Finally, I would like to thank two Mrs Crosses — my wife and my mother — for putting up with this eccentric behaviour, the unusual hours, and for their patience. For this book my mother provided the shove I needed to start and my wife the assistance with the production. I do hope you enjoy the book.

David Cross
Brentwood
March 2005

Left: Father and sons Sheridan (centre) and David (right) on a photographic outing, note the Linhof beside Derek ready for action (inset) the author today.

Above: Shed shots do not feature greatly amongst the Derek Cross collection. This photograph, taken on 17 September 1972 at Eastfield depot in Glasgow, provides an exception. Derek's notes refer to an open day at the largest diesel depot in Scotland with, at that time, an allocation of more than 100 locomotives. Pictured all cleaned up for the event are 'Deltic' No 9021 *Argyll and Sutherland Highlander*, Class 27 No 5362 and Class 37 No 6848. All these locomotives and their respective sisters had a long association with Scotland. The 'Deltic' and the Class 27 were withdrawn and disposed of by the mid-1980s; however, the Class 37 was converted and re-engined, becoming No 37902 and it remains intact in Nottinghamshire, although stored today some 42 years after being constructed at Vulcan Foundry in 1963. Interestingly, the Eastfield depot site has just been reopened as a new DMU depot. *Derek Cross*

Right: Although the Edinburgh–Glasgow 'high-speed' service, introduced in 1971, was supposed to be in the hands of BRCW Class 27s this was not always the case. Derek has pictures of Classes 25, 27 and 37 on these services in various combinations. Passing Greenhill Lower Junction in September 1972 we see a pair of Class 25s involved, with No 7581 at the front and No 7590 on the rear of the six-coach formation. The train is the 13.00 Edinburgh to Glasgow service diverted that day due to engineering work just outside Glasgow. That Sunday the 'high-speed' timing of 47 minutes for 45 miles would have been extended. In all probability both the locomotives would have been back on mixed freight in central Scotland later in the week. Both locomotives later returned to English sheds, to be withdrawn from Crewe Diesel depot in the mid-1980s. *Derek Cross*

Left: Class 27s on Mk3 coaching stock were not common. Pictured, however, on 15 August 1976 we see No 27108 roaring out of Glasgow Central station with the empty stock of the recently arrived 'Royal Scot' from London Euston. The empty stock would be taken the three or so miles to the carriage sheds at Polmadie for servicing. These sidings, adjacent to the old steam shed at Polmadie (66A), had by the 1970s taken over from a number of other passenger rolling stock yards in south Glasgow. Sadly, interesting-sounding names such as Bellahouston, Smithy Lye and Rutherglen had all been superseded by the single servicing facility. The advent of diesel multiple-units (DMUs), more intensive diagrams and less excursion traffic all contributed to this.

No 27108, the former D5396, had started life at Cricklewood in north London in 1962 but worked much of its life in Scotland, being withdrawn from Eastfield depot in 1987. *Derek Cross*

Above right: The diesel multiple-unit was and, again in more modern times, is the main means of rail passenger transport in Scotland. Pictured passing Cadder Yard near Bishopbriggs is one of the early Swindon-built diesel units on a Glasgow to Edinburgh service. These units had been built in 1957 and later became Class 126.

Unusually the formation has three driving trailers, being the first, second and sixth vehicles. The date was April 1971 and as these 'Inter-City' DMUs were about to be replaced by the push-pull Class 27 service, maintenance and repairs were perhaps not as comprehensive as they had been, leading to the mixed formation.

One such unit has been preserved and is being restored, appropriately at nearby Bo'ness, home of the Scottish Railway Preservation Society. It is well worth a visit to see many of the classes featured in this 'Colour Portfolio' of Scottish diesels. *Derek Cross*

Right: Cadder was a surprisingly rural location for a marshalling yard and a favourite location of Derek in the central belt of Scotland. With only fields and a tractor in the distance, it is difficult to believe this site is only 6 miles from Queen Street station in central Glasgow.

Pictured is a test train (1Z91) in preparation for the Class 27 push-pull service (which began later in 1971) passing Cadder, heading west towards Glasgow. The train would have started from Haymarket just outside Edinburgh. Heading the train is BRCW (Birmingham Railway Carriage & Wagon Co) Type 2 No 5411 with sister locomotive No 5404 at the rear. No 5411 had lost its 'D' prefix by this time and, if we count these as two numbers, the locomotive had a further three numbers during its life making a total of five identities in a working life of just under 24 years. The locomotive was withdrawn from Inverness shed in May 1986.

The concept of push-pull operations (or top and tail as it later became known) on the Glasgow–Edinburgh main line was to a degree forced upon the Scottish Region by much improved road competition (the M8!) and the fact that the Swindon DMUs from 1957 were becoming life expired after some 14 years in traffic. *Derek Cross*

Left: On 12 May 1970 'Peak' Class 46 No D139 sets off from Glasgow Central station with train 1E31, the afternoon departure to Sheffield. For many years there had always been a twice-daily service from Glasgow (originally St Enoch station, which closed in 1966) to St Pancras via the ex-Glasgow & South Western Railway (GSWR) main line, the Settle & Carlisle and the Midland main line. Gradually this service was contracted to Leeds and then Sheffield and finally done away with altogether. It was briefly revived in the 1990s as a DMU service between Leeds and Glasgow, but this too has now been discontinued. The changing nature of our railway now means that to go from Glasgow Central to Leeds it is faster and more comfortable to travel via Carstairs, Edinburgh and York than to travel the more conventional route that the picture illustrates from 35 years ago.

No D139 became the second Class 46, No 46002, when renumbered in February 1974. It remained in traffic until September 1987 when it was finally withdrawn from Gateshead depot. *Derek Cross*

Above: Having just passed through the Cumbernauld Glen, a Rail Blue Class 101 DMU sets off down Cumbernauld Bank towards Glasgow. The picture was taken on Sunday, 17 September 1972 and the train was an Edinburgh to Glasgow six-car semi-fast service.

The Class 101 diesel units were standard fare for many suburban lines in Scotland once steam disappeared. Geographically they covered virtually all of Scotland for many years. Over 750 were built between 1956 and 1959 by Metropolitan-Cammell at Washwood Heath in Birmingham, and the last of the class were only withdrawn from the Manchester area in 2003 — one of them had a Scottish livery, emphasising the strong Scottish connection. Over 40 are now preserved, a fact which tells its own story. These units generally, and in Scotland in particular, gave excellent service. *Derek Cross*

Left: Usually the preserve of Class 27s, this picture of No 7590 proves that occasionally Class 25s and Class 37s were used on the Edinburgh–Glasgow high-speed service.

The history behind this push-pull service introduced in 1971 was that the 1957 Swindon-built Class 126 DMUs had done 14 years' work and needed either refurbishment or replacement. Lack of speed, age and passenger comforts led the operating authorities to take the brave decision to go for the push-pull option. The basic needs of quick turnaround and operational flexibility could be catered for by using an engine at each end. Perhaps strangely, after a successful trial with a Class 37 the decision was taken to go with a Class 27 at each end of a six-coach formation.

No 7590, with another Class 25 at the rear of the train, heads towards Edinburgh with the Kilsyth hills in the background. *Derek Cross*

Below: Falkirk is a surprisingly big town, with a population of some 144,000. It boasts two stations, namely Falkirk High and the one pictured here, Falkirk Grahamston. Photographed passing through Grahamston station are a pair of Sulzer-powered Type 2s — BR-built No 5130 and BRCW No 5338 — with the afternoon Edinburgh–Inverness working. The date is 7 September 1971.

The headlights on the front locomotive (unusual in those days), identify No 5130 as an Inverness-allocated (60A) Highland lines engine. These locomotives all had headlights fitted to help drivers on the rural lines in the Highlands of Scotland, where they spent much of their careers. New to Inverness in 1960, No 5130 was actually withdrawn from Haymarket at the end of 1976 but virtually its entire 16-year life had been spent in the north. No D5338, although withdrawn in the early 1990s, has been preserved and is presently being restored to working order in Wales, a part of the UK Class 26s never reached in BR service! *David Cross*

Perhaps one of the most photographed Anglo-Scottish trains was 5M20, the 10.15 empty vans from Perth to Manchester, Red Bank. The attraction of this train was the unpredictability of the motive power that Scottish control might provide. Seen leaving Stirling on 14 June 1979 is ETH-fitted Class 47 No 47706 *Strathclyde*, itself unusual motive power for the working, which conveyed empty newspaper vans back to Manchester.

No 47706 (the former D1936, new to Cardiff Canton in 1966) was one of 17 Class 47s ultimately converted for push-pull use in Scotland from 1979. These were for use on the main Scottish InterCity routes from Glasgow to Edinburgh and later to Aberdeen. It is therefore slightly unusual to see a specially converted and dedicated passenger locomotive on a parcels train, but that was the Red Bank! Unusually, unlike its companion locomotives, the nameplate 'Strathclyde' was only carried until April 1986. This nameplate can now be seen in the Scottish Transport Museum at the Kelvin Hall in Glasgow.

No 47706 and its companions with DBSOs (Driver Brake Standard Open) formed the basis of Scottish main-line passenger services for 10 years from 1979, before giving way to newer technology and units. Some Class 47/7 locomotives made their way south to Network SouthEast and others to the parcels sector. A handful remain in traffic in 2005. *Les Riley*

Pictured passing south through Gleneagles station on 14 June 1979 is English Electric Class 40 No 40150. The train is the 4E86 13.50 Freightliner service from Aberdeen to London, King's Cross Freightliner Terminal. In those early days of containerisation Freightliner ran an extensive network of domestic intermodal services with 20ft-, 30ft- and 40ft-long containers. These services covered much of the country, with Freightliner depots in Aberdeen, Dudley, Glasgow Gushetfaulds and Willesden. These depots were in addition to the inland ports at Leeds, Manchester, Coatbridge and Birmingham and, of course, the big international container ports at Felixstowe, Southampton and on the Thames, which make up the bulk of business for Freightliner at the start of the 21st century. Sadly, as the 1980s progressed the domestic traffic waned and many depots closed, including both Aberdeen and King's Cross.

No 40150, new to York as D350 in June 1961, remained in traffic until almost the end of the service life of the class, being withdrawn from Carlisle Kingmoor in January 1985. *Les Riley*

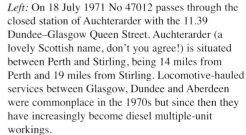

Left: On 18 July 1971 No 47012 passes through the closed station of Auchterarder with the 11.39 Dundee–Glasgow Queen Street. Auchterarder (a lovely Scottish name, don't you agree!) is situated between Perth and Stirling, being 14 miles from Perth and 19 miles from Stirling. Locomotive-hauled services between Glasgow, Dundee and Aberdeen were commonplace in the 1970s but since then they have increasingly become diesel multiple-unit workings.

Locomotive No 47012 was built by Brush as D1539 and entered service in 1963 at Sheffield Darnall shed (41A). Unusually, the locomotive was also later withdrawn from a Sheffield shed — Tinsley in December 1989. This Brush Type 4 had a working life of 26 years whilst others of the class built the following year (1964) are still soldiering on in traffic today, some 41 years later. The class has had a very long withdrawal period, some parts of the modern railway still being unable to do without these Brush thoroughbreds, it seems. *Les Riley*

Left: The wonderful airy sprawling junction station at Perth sees Class 25 No 25044 standing at the southbound platform awaiting departure time. The train is the 2T38 15.57 Dundee Tay Bridge–Glasgow Queen Street semi-fast. The date is 11 June 1979.

The distance from Dundee to Glasgow is 83 miles, and these semi-fasts had leisurely timings (about 100 minutes for the journey), often, as here at Perth, having to wait time in stations.

No 25044, originally D5194, entered traffic in May 1963, allocated to Derby. During a working life of just over 20 years it and other members of the class often crossed the border and had periods based at English and Scottish sheds. Last allocated to Carlisle Kingmoor, the locomotive was withdrawn in July 1985 and scrapped at Doncaster the following year.

Perth, as well as being an excellent photographic location, was an interesting station with something always going on, be it passenger, parcels, freight or engineering trains, in all directions to Inverness, Dundee, Aberdeen, Glasgow, Edinburgh and Carlisle. *Les Riley*

The missing semaphore arm tells its own sad story of the demise of a major junction. Stanley Junction, just north of Perth, is beginning to show signs of decay, as revealed by the encroaching weeds and dilapidated platelayers' hut.

Pictured in late summer 1973 heading north on a Glasgow–Inverness express (1N20) is a pair of Class 26s, Nos 5334 and 5327. The train is about to swing away to the right on to the Highland main line, with the next stop being Dunkeld & Birnam. By this time the purpose of the junction had been much reduced. The former main line to Aberdeen via Kinnaber Junction had closed to passengers from 4 September 1967 to become a freight-only branch to Forfar. This, in turn, closed from 5 June 1982, the last train being a railtour hauled by No 40143. *Derek Cross*

In the good old days when locomotive-hauled services ruled Scotland two Class 26s, No 5331 leading 5330, arrive at Newtonmore. The station on 8 August 1973 looks a picture, with semaphore signals, the old Highland Railway signalbox, the goods shed, the coal yard in use and a single litter-free flower bed. Sadly, only a single passenger awaits the arrival of the Inverness–Glasgow express.

Inverness to Glasgow is a deceptively long distance, some 180 miles, and often the journey took around four hours. Already 50 miles from Inverness, the last stop would have been Kingussie and the next one Dalwhinnie. Perth is 68 miles further south and Glasgow about the same distance again beyond Perth.

Beautifully engineered and with endless photographic opportunities, the Highland main line was a great favourite of Derek, given half decent weather! For this picture taken on 18 August 1973, I leave you to decide. *Derek Cross*

What a lovely Highland Railway signalbox at Aviemore South in the late 1960s!

Engaged in lengthy shunting operations is BRCW Type 2 No D5344, the penultimate member of the class and recently reliveried from green to blue. The locomotive later became 26044 under the TOPS renumbering scheme in April 1974 and remained in service a further 10 years until being withdrawn from Inverness depot in 1984.

Aviemore in days gone by had been a large junction with lines serving (clockwise) Inverness, Forres, Craigellachie, Keith and Aberdeen, as well as Perth, Glasgow, Edinburgh and, of course, London direct. Even today Aviemore boasts two named trains each day, serving both the East Coast main line to King's Cross and the West Coast route to Euston.

Just five years earlier, in the 1965 timetable, Aviemore had local services to Inverness via Nairn and Elgin via Boat of Garten. All these branches have closed, but the Strathspey Railway does operate diesel and steam services along the line towards Boat of Garten from the north end of Aviemore station.
Derek Cross

Left: A mile east of Inverness, with the Moray Firth and the Black Isle in the background, this photograph was taken during the transition years from steam to diesel. On the evening of 16 April 1968, we see maroon and blue and grey coaching stock as well as the red mail van, with one blue and one green locomotive on the evening departure to Glasgow and Edinburgh as the 13-coach formation leaves Inverness. In the background is the Aberdeen–Inverness line.

The train is hauled by BRCW Type 2s (later Class 26) Nos D5343 in blue and D5334 in green. Unusually, D5343 has the BR double-arrow symbol (still much in evidence today on road signs and rail tickets 10 years after BR ended!) painted on the locomotive doors.

Both locomotives had long associations with the Highland lines and remained in service until the 1980s, when Class 47s took over the bulk of their main-line

duties. Today, all these services are diesel multiple-units, with the exception of the sleeping car service to and from London Euston. *Derek Cross*

Above: Gone, all gone! Since this photograph was taken on 19 September 1973 everything in this picture (save perhaps the fisherman) has gone. First, the locomotive, Class 40 No 363, *en route* from Inverness to Muir of Ord to collect a grain train, was scrapped at the Berry yard in Leicester in 1987, after a working life of 21 years (1961-82). Secondly, the stone viaduct over the River Ness just north of the Highland capital was itself washed away in a flood during the night of 7 February 1989. How quickly the railway scene changes! Even the grain train that the locomotive was going to collect is no longer part of the modern freight railway. *Derek Cross*

No apologies for a special train I'm afraid, as the sight of a pair of Class 24s on the Kyle line alongside the beautiful Loch Carron in good weather is worth inclusion. The only slight difference from normal operations is the length of the train, on this occasion a Wirral Railway Circle Special from Crewe to Kyle of Lochalsh on 22 September 1973. The 63 miles of single line from Dingwall to Kyle of Lochalsh runs alongside Loch Carron for 13 miles, one of the most scenic stretches of railway in Scotland.

Although the Class 24s were very common on the Kyle and other far north lines the two locomotives on the train have very different backgrounds. The leading locomotive, No 5129, was for a long time an Inverness locomotive, headlight-fitted and very common in the Highlands. The train engine, however, No 5113, was not a regular Highland lines visitor. As No D5113 the last of 20 locomotives built at Darlington (as opposed to Derby or Crewe), in January 1961, it was allocated new to Gateshead, where these locomotives replaced '9Fs' on the legendary Tyne Dock iron ore workings. Without route indicators or headlights, this locomotive must have been approaching the end of its life when it reached the Kyle line. The locomotives were coincidentally withdrawn from the same shed (Haymarket) in the same month (December 1976) and cut up at BREL, Doncaster, the following year.
Derek Cross

Creeping along the southern shore of Loch Carron is BRCW No 5330 on a Kyle of Lochalsh to Inverness service in April 1971. The train has just emerged from the recently completed tunnel for the railway and the A890 road on the very edge of the loch. After repeated rock falls from the cliffs on the left-hand side British Rail had decided to build the tunnel to protect the track and road.

Even the passenger trains along this highly scenic stretch did not go very fast and I recall more than once racing in Derek's Rover 2000 along the side of the loch from one photographic spot to another. As his car was dark blue, Derek thought he could get away with such speeds! You may not get away with those speeds today but it was great fun.
Derek Cross

On 6 April 1971 the terminus of Kyle of Lochalsh sees BR Sulzer No D5128 in the platform with a parcels service to Inverness. The background is as interesting as the main subject. Furthest away, the Isle of Skye, with the bulk of Ben na Caillich, dominates the background, in the other platform the 11.20 passenger train is waiting to depart for Inverness and, finally, the single-deck bus is leaving the station en route to Glenelg.

The steam-age shedplate 60A, albeit painted yellow, on the front of the locomotive, above the Highland lines' headlight, denotes No D5128 was allocated to Inverness Lochgorm shed. Built at Derby and new to Inverness depot in August 1960, a great part of its 16-year working life was spent on the lines to and from the far north. The locomotive was withdrawn from Haymarket depot in Edinburgh in July 1976.

Although the train appears to be a parcels, it was also sometimes used to convey goods wagons and so perhaps could be deemed to be a mixed train.
Derek Cross

With more than 40 wagons in tow, BRCW Type 2 No D5340 sets off from Kyle of Lochalsh for Inverness, Millburn Yard. Pictured in the spring of 1968, near the hamlet of Drumbuie, the train has not yet got to the first passenger station heading east out of Kyle, at Duirinish, some four miles distant.

The variety of vans depicts the wide range of freight that British Rail handled in those days with general cargo vans, cattle wagons, oil tanks and an engineer's ballast wagon, most of which is lost from rail in this part of Scotland today. Before the bridge from Kyle of Lochalsh to Skye was built all the cargo for Skye tended to go to Kyle of Lochalsh and forward to Kyleakin by ferry, which perhaps explains the number of the return empties on the train.

The locomotive, recently repainted in Rail Blue, is 1959-built Class 26 No D5340, another long-term Highland lines' locomotive. *Derek Cross*

Class 26 No D5330 sets off from Kyle of Lochalsh for Inverness in April 1971. The extensive nature of the yards on both sides of the passenger station are clearly visible.

Next to the locomotive is a four-wheeled CCT (Covered Carriage Truck) van, fairly common for mail and parcels on the Kyle line at this time in the early 1970s. I have also seen bicycles being loaded into the CCT, with the cyclists, who were on holiday in western Scotland and the Hebrides.

No D5330 was new to Scotland (Edinburgh Haymarket) in 1960 and spent its entire working life in the country until withdrawal from Inverness depot in March 1985. I can still hear the distinctive engine noise so characteristic of this class. *Derek Cross*

Approaching the first station out of Kyle, at Duirinish, is Sulzer Type 2 No D5128 on the Kyle of Lochalsh–Inverness goods and parcels, carrying a mixture of bogie vans and four-wheel vans as well as a brake van. Following the morning passenger service, this parcels/freight would go through to Inverness, stopping as necessary, with Dingwall being the major station on the route. Just north of Dingwall (19 miles before Inverness), the long-distance branches to Kyle of Lochalsh and the far north line to Thurso and Wick diverge.

BR/Sulzer No D5128 was very common on these lines, and so often photographed by Derek that he decided to buy a kit of a Class 24/1, assemble it and paint it as D5128. This was most out of character and I'm not sure where the patience came from! I was so surprised, that I kept this OO gauge model, and still have it today. *Derek Cross*

Below: The late 1970s saw the stranglehold that Classes 24 and 26 had had on the far north lines broken by the arrival of the more powerful Class 37s. These more reliable and stronger locomotives were a hit with the train crews and soon made these long-distance branch lines their own. Indeed, members of the class still cling on to selected passenger duties on the West Highland line.

This locomotive, No 37025, had been new to Stratford in late 1961 and gradually worked north, being allocated to Tees in 1976 and to Glasgow Eastfield by the time this picture was taken on 29 May 1982. The locomotive is now preserved in Scotland at Bo'ness and was re-started in January 2005. The train is the morning Kyle of Lochalsh–Inverness service, pictured near Duncraig shortly after leaving Kyle of Lochalsh, with the Isle of Skye in the background. *Derek Cross*

Right: Movement of logs came late to the West Highland but thankfully still forms the backbone of rail freight in this part of Scotland today. The log traffic is nowadays loaded in the yard adjacent to Crianlarich Upper station but back in 1971 the logs were loaded in the Lower station yard, which was part of the former Oban main line through Glen Ogle to Dunblane. By 5 April 1971 the old main line was closed (by a catastrophic landslide) and the truncated branch used to Crianlarich Lower yard to load timber. Here we see Class 27 No 5355. Having pulled the timber train from Crianlarich Lower locomotive-first towards Oban then once over the junction to Crianlarich Upper, it would then propel the loaded train (seen here) up the hill to join the West Highland line in Crianlarich Upper. The train would then set off over the West Highland line to its destination, the vast paper mill at Corpach, some three miles outside Fort William on the Mallaig extension. *David Cross*

Below: Class 27 No 5369 has just arrived in the platform at Crianlarich Upper with an Oban–Glasgow express. Alongside the station is another Class 27 locomotive shunting in the yard. The yard seems to be a mixture of engineers' vehicles and timber wagons. At this stage in the spring of 1971 all West Highland workings were dominated by these 1,250hp Class 27 locomotives, all based at Eastfield depot in Glasgow (once the famous 65A, later ED, then closed and now in 2005 reopened for DMUs).

These Type 2s did some excellent work on the West Highland line, having taken over from the less reliable Class 21/29 North British Locomotive Co (NBL) locomotives of the D61xx series. In turn, the '27s' gave way to the bigger and more powerful Class 37s, half a dozen of which are today still involved with the sleeping car service and excursion traffic over the West Highland line. *Derek Cross*

Right: Pulling into the pretty wayside station of Dalmally is No 27112 on 5 May 1979. Dalmally is 25 miles east of Oban and the second crossing point heading east out of the west coast port. Before reaching Dalmally, the Oban branch passes through the rugged pass of Brander, which has signals which are always in the off position unless rock falls trigger the wire that links them to each other. After Dalmally the Oban branch runs through Tyndrum to Crianlarich, 18 miles away, where it joins the West Highland line.

The station is very photogenic in both directions and pictured here is train IT32, the 12.20 Oban to Glasgow Queen Street. In all likelihood, a crossing with a down train to Oban would take place, giving even greater scope for photography. Although it was May, Les Riley, the photographer, has been lucky enough to capture some snow still lying on Ben Evnaich (988m) high above the station. *Les Riley*

Right: A real winter scene on the West Highland line — except it is the end of March, 22 March 1980 to be precise!

Pictured sitting at the station platform at Tulloch is the 07.00 Mallaig–Glasgow service (via Fort William). The snow is falling quite heavily and with the 'wild' section of the West Highland line still to come there is probably some apprehension on the footplate, although a westbound freight in the other platform appears to have successfully negotiated the 47 miles from Crianlarich over Rannoch Moor.

The train is hauled by Class 27 No 27040, the former D5402 of Eastfield depot. The locomotive would remain in traffic for a further six years before being scrapped at, unusually, Thornton Junction in April 1987. *Les Riley*

It is spring in the beautiful Monessie Gorge between Roy Bridge and Tulloch at the western end of the West Highland line. The train is the Fort William–London service that still runs today (still with ageing diesel traction in the shape of Class 37s) six days a week, conveying both day coaches and sleeping cars.

Seen here in early April 1968 are a pair of the short-lived North British Locomotive Co's Class 29s climbing up through the gorge, which is some 15 miles out of Fort William. The locomotives, Nos D6129 and D6124, shared very similar careers. Both were new to Ipswich, then 32B, within a month of each other in autumn 1959. Their stay on the Great Eastern was short before they emigrated to Scotland. At that stage they were Class 21s. Again within a month of each other they were re-engined and converted to Class 29s in March and April 1967. Both were withdrawn in December 1971, finally being scrapped at BREL Glasgow during the summer of 1972. *Derek Cross*

Pictured in the old station (now a dual carriageway!) in Fort William is BRCW Class 27 No D5369 about to set off to Mallaig. The date is April 1971.

The 41-mile branch to Mallaig, known as the Mallaig extension, is arguably one of the most scenic lines in the UK, with beautiful countryside and spectacular engineering. There are eight intermediate stops, at Banavie, Corpach, Loch Eil, Glenfinnan, Lochailort, Beasdale, Arisaig and Morar. It is a line well worth the distance travelled (164 miles from Glasgow to Mallaig) and one I never tire of visiting.

No D5369 became 27023 and was withdrawn from traffic from Haymarket depot in Edinburgh in May 1986. It was another member of the 31 Class 27s cut up at the Vic Berry yard in Leicester — itself now a housing development.
Derek Cross

Left: Storming away from the station stop at Lochailort, 15 miles from its destination at Mallaig, is the 10.03 Fort William–Mallaig. The picture was taken on 16 July 1982 and, perhaps unusually, the train was running during an ASLEF dispute.

The locomotive is Class 37 No 37047 *Loch Lomond*, then very much a West Highland locomotive based at Eastfield in Glasgow. Later, the locomotive was de-named and transferred 'down South', becoming No 37354 when replaced on the West Highland by electrically heated Class 37/4s.

We often travelled on these locomotive-hauled trains on the Mallaig extension and trundling along the single line in no great hurry, looking at the beautiful scenery from the picture window of a Mk 1, was enchanting. It was something any lover of railways would remember. *Les Riley*

Below: Cupar, Fife (as opposed to Coupar Angus), on 18 March 1972 sees Class 40 No 364 arriving with an Aberdeen–Edinburgh express. Cupar is located 15 miles south of Dundee and some 34 miles north of the Forth Bridge at Queensferry.

Already in blue livery it would be two more years before No 364 became 40164 in September 1974. A Scottish Region locomotive from new in 1961, virtually all of its working life was spent in Scotland. Interestingly, I read the other day that this locomotive, as 40164, had carried an unofficial name 'Lismore' towards the end of its life. During the 1980s, when BR had either a no-name policy or a miserable naming policy, a number of unofficial names began to appear, tastefully applied in paint on the locomotives. About 300 locomotives were named in this way, including, I'm told, 40164 and just seven other Class 40 locomotives … Were they photographed? No 40164 was withdrawn from Crewe in July 1983. *David Cross*

This photograph was taken immediately west of Dundee Tay Bridge station. On the left we can see the old Dundee Tay Bridge steam shed and some typical Scottish tenement housing, whilst on the right the viaduct up onto the Tay Bridge can be seen. The date is 19 April 1972.

The train coming towards the camera is an Aberdeen–Glasgow express hauled by Class 40 No 369 of Haymarket shed in Edinburgh. Heading in the opposite direction is a Glasgow Queen Street–Dundee service about to arrive at its destination, hauled by Glasgow Eastfield-based Class 27 No D5366.

I am pleased to include this picture of Dundee because, for a large city with a varied railway network, good pictures at Dundee are hard to find. *Derek Cross*

Scotland has always had a variety of shunting locomotives. In steam days both on BR and within the industrial sector (National Coal Board etc) there was a great variety of shunting locomotives or 'Pugs' as they were more commonly known in Scotland.

As steam gave way to diesel a new generation of diesel shunters grew up in Scotland. North British in Glasgow and Andrew Barclay in Kilmarnock built hundreds of shunters through the 1950s and 1960s, some of which did not last very long at all. The 72-strong NBL 'D2708' class, for example, did not last long enough for any of its members to receive a TOPS number.

The 1958 Andrew Barclay class of 0-6-0 diesel shunters, which became Class 06, fared better. Of the 34 built, most worked in Scotland and 10 of these lasted in traffic long enough to have TOPS numbers — 06001 (D2413) to 06010 (D2444) in 1974/5. Pictured here is No 06006 (former D2423), caught shunting grain wagons behind Ferryhill depot in Aberdeen on 24 October 1976. This locomotive lasted a further four years in traffic before being withdrawn from Dundee depot in June 1980, ultimately being scrapped there in 1983.
Derek Cross

Left: Typical of many stations in the north of Scotland, Peterhead was similar to both Wick and Thurso, with a short, dark, covered start to the platform. Sadly, on the day this photograph was taken, 5 September 1970, the station would never be required again as this two-coach special was to be the last passenger train from this town in the far northeastern corner of Scotland. Peterhead is probably more famous for its high-security prison or its fishing fleet than for its railways, so it was no real surprise that towards the end of the Beeching era the proverbial axe caught up with the town.

Peterhead's passenger rail service had been four trains each way per day to Aberdeen, some 44 miles away, with a change at Maud Junction to the direct service from Aberdeen to Fraserburgh.

BRCW Class 26 No D5307 had seen initial service on the Great Northern section out of King's Cross when new to Hornsey (34B) at the end of 1958. Soon afterwards it was transferred to the Scottish Region. Later the locomotive was renumbered out of sequence to 26020 in April 1974. It was withdrawn in January 1977. *Derek Cross*

Above: The single-line branch leaving the East Coast main line (ECML) on the left to North Berwick tells us the picture is at Drem Junction. The express from King's Cross is only a few minutes from its destination at Edinburgh Waverley. At the head of 1S32, a train made up of ETH Mk 2d coaching stock, is the second-built of the 512-strong Class 47, No D1501. It was delivered new to Finsbury Park (34G) in November 1962 and with other early Class 47s and the 'Deltics' provided motive power on the ECML for nearly 20 years. The locomotive is today preserved at the Midland Railway Centre, Butterley in Derbyshire.

The ECML is now electrified and the convenient footbridge from which the picture was taken and the semaphore signals are all consigned to history. Just 18 miles from Edinburgh Waverley, Drem, although a rural location, could now be described as the Edinburgh commuter belt. As I write, there is renewed interest in the North Berwick branch with the return of locomotive-hauled services on the branch using 5,000hp electric locomotives. *Derek Cross*

A typical 1970s scene on the East Coast main line into Scotland. Pictured just west of Dunbar, which can be seen in the background, is the down 'Flying Scotsman' (1S17), the 10.00 from London King's Cross to Edinburgh Waverley. The motive power, typically, is one of the 22 'Deltics' that hauled the top-link expresses on the ECML at that time. The locomotive is No 9019 *Royal Highland Fusilier*, a particular favourite of Derek's. He felt that, of all the 'Deltics', this one followed him around, with pictures at King's Cross, Inverness, Beattock and here on the East Coast main line in Scotland.

No 9019 was delivered new to Haymarket in December 1961 and remained in traffic for almost 20 years, being withdrawn from York shed in December 1981. Now owned by the Deltic Preservation Society, it is currently resident at Barrow Hill in Derbyshire and is presently being overhauled. It has seen a further return to main line running later in 2005.
Derek Cross

Millerhill Yard, on the outskirts of Edinburgh, was obsolete more or less by the time it was completed in the 1960s. A number of 'super' marshalling yards were set up at that time to allow a more efficient rail freight operation. These included Kingmoor in Carlisle, Tinsley in Sheffield and Millerhill for Scotland. At the same time the explosion of commercial road freight transport was taking place and soon these modern yards were not being used as much as was intended. The lack of freight traffic was accelerated by the closure of the very nearby Waverley route to Carlisle via Hawick in 1969.

However, the yard was (and remains) partly in use. On 7 September 1971 we see two-tone-green BR/Sulzer Type 2 No 5071 of Haymarket (64B) depot engaged in shunting operations, with the shunter walking on the left-hand side of the train. No D5071 was new to March in February 1960 and lasted in traffic until August 1975, when it was withdrawn from Haymarket. The locomotive was disposed of at BREL Doncaster in January 1977.

In the background can be seen the old Edinburgh-Glasgow DMUs stored in the yard. *David Cross*

Left: Creeping through Princes Street Gardens on the approach to Edinburgh Waverley station on 4 May 1968 is Class 47 No D1968. The train, an Aberdeen–Edinburgh express, is three minutes away from its journey's end.

Built at Crewe in October 1965, No D1968 was the first of a small group of nine Class 47s (D1968-76) allocated from new to Haymarket. Although many other Class 47s would later be allocated to sheds in Scotland (Glasgow Eastfield, Inverness and Haymarket), these nine were the only examples allocated to the Scottish Region from new. This locomotive spent much of its working life in Scotland and was one of those converted to Class 47/7 in 1979, emerging from Crewe works in June of that year as No 47708 and named *Waverley*. Later, it transferred to Waterloo–Exeter services and was withdrawn in April 1995 then scrapped at Crewe in August the same year. *Derek Cross*

Right: Passing the signalbox, on the right, which controlled one end of Waverley station in Edinburgh, is the 17.00 high-speed service to Glasgow Queen Street. The date is 6 June 1971. The famous bridges, which link the Old and New Town, are very visible in the background and unusually without a maroon and white Edinburgh Corporation bus in this picture.

Leading the six-coach formation to Glasgow is BRCW Type 2 No 5408 with another Type 2, No 5413, at the rear of the train. The Class 27s performed well on these demanding and intensively diagrammed push-pull operations. They had not been designed for these short high-speed workings but coped well, with several reported as exceeding the 90mph speed limit.

Altogether 12 of the class were converted at Glasgow and Derby workshops. Of the two locomotives featured here, both were Smethwick-built, near Birmingham, and both, after a life in Scotland, met their end in Leicester in July 1987.

In the background a Class 40, No D366, is in the platform ready to depart with an express to Aberdeen. *Derek Cross*

43

Left: Train 1E83, the 14.15 Edinburgh–Newcastle stopper, was one almost guaranteed to be completely unpredictable in terms of motive power. Derek took pictures of this service with 'Deltics', Class 47s, Class 46s, Class 40s, Class 25s and, here on 3 June 1972, an English Electric Type 3 Class 37.

Pictured on the northern approach to Penmanshiel Tunnel is No D6781. New to Hull Dairycoates depot 10 years earlier, in June 1962, the locomotive later became a dedicated Highland lines' locomotive as No 37081 *Loch Long* and, later still, a freight locomotive as No 37797. It is still extant in the ownership of EWS, albeit withdrawn at Toton.

Sadly, seven years later on 17 March 1979 part of the tunnel collapsed and two railway workers lost their lives. The old tunnel was sealed up, in part as a tomb, and a new deviation officially opened on 20 August 1979. *Derek Cross*

Right: For years the smoky DMU was the workhorse of the Scottish suburban networks. Indeed, new-generation DMUs continue to form the basis of the region's passenger services today.

Although Derek was neither very keen on DMUs, nor very knowledgeable about them, he recorded shots of them at work all over Scotland. Pictured emerging from the Mound Tunnel in June 1971 is a Class 101 three-car unit in Rail Blue livery, setting off on a service from Edinburgh Waverley to Kirkcaldy in Fife. This section of line is now electrified to Haymarket and onto the WCML via Carstairs. *Derek Cross*

We have in this picture crept over the border to England. Although Berwick-upon-Tweed is on the north bank of the River Tweed, it is still a Northumbrian town, and the England/Scotland border is some four miles north, crossed by the East Coast main line at Marshall Meadows.

Pictured at the south end of the island platform at Berwick-upon-Tweed is

'Peak' Class 45 No 20. The train is the 1E27 evening Edinburgh–Leeds service, and No 20 is on its way back to its home depot of Leeds Holbeck. Later, No 20 became 45013 and remained in traffic as a non-electric-heating locomotive until April 1987, when it was withdrawn from Tinsley depot in Sheffield.

The photograph was taken at the end of May 1972. *David Cross*

Hauling a scheduled car train from Bathgate to the Eastern Region, EE Type 3 No 6728 climbs the final yards to the summit at Grantshouse between Dunbar and Berwick-upon-Tweed on 27 June 1970. There were two car-manufacturing plants in Scotland at the time, at Bathgate in the east and Linwood, near Paisley, in the west. These 1970s Anglo-Scottish car trains were very different from those of today, although this one seems not very well loaded.

The picture was taken from the steps of Grantshouse signalbox. As well as a block section, Grantshouse had both up and down loops and a crossover between the main lines. The station itself had closed to passengers on 4 May 1964.

No 6728 later became No 37505, a freight locomotive, and is currently stored in Ayr, where Derek lived and had his Scottish base for many years. The locomotive is one of a handful of Class 37s named after Railfreight customers, No 37505 becoming *British Steel Workington*. *Derek Cross*

Below: Here is 1E83 again, the 14.15 Edinburgh to Newcastle semi-fast, with yet another locomotive. This time, in April 1972, we see an English Electric Class 40, No 281, on the service just six miles into the journey to Newcastle, at the eastern end of Millerhill yard near Monktonhall Junction; the next stop will be Prestonpans.

No D281 was new to York shed in 1960 and spent much of its working life on the Eastern and Scottish regions, although the locomotive was withdrawn from an LMR shed at Manchester, Longsight in February 1983, being cut up at BREL Doncaster the following year.

The clean locomotive, spring sunshine and matching coaching stock evoke a typical BR locomotive-hauled passenger train in Scotland in the 1970s. *Derek Cross*

Right: 27 June 1970 sees a two-car Gloucester RCW DMU set sitting in the, by then, single platform at the old station at North Berwick.

The branch to North Berwick (from Drem) is now electrified and flourishes both as a commuter line to Edinburgh and Haymarket and as a railhead to some of the best golf links in Scotland. Nearby Muirfield at Gullane is a famous Open Championship course.

The North Berwick branch is back in the railway press, courtesy of Class 90 electric locomotives and modern, air-conditioned carriages that provide users of the line with much better accommodation than they have ever had — a huge advance on the DMU pictured here.

The new station at North Berwick has a straight platform and, from memory, is a few hundred yards further inland than the old station, which once had two platforms. *Derek Cross*

Above: For a class of locomotive, the majority of which were commissioned in 1963/4, to be in storage in Millerhill yard by March 1972 really says it all. The Clayton Type 1s were one of a number of diesel classes introduced in a hurry as part of the 1955 BR Modernisation Plan. Many of these were not very successful and, in terms of hours worked, the 'Claytons' were at the low end. They were concentrated in Scotland and the northeast of England and tended to work in pairs to achieve sufficient power. By 1972 large numbers of the class were either withdrawn or in store at Millerhill near Edinburgh and at the old steam sheds at Polmadie (in Glasgow) and Ardrossan.

Pictured here from right to left are green and blue locomotives, in sequence, Nos 8597, 8583, 8528, 8579 and 8593. All had been withdrawn from Scottish sheds in September and October 1971 and, after their spell here in Millerhill yard, all were scrapped at Glasgow works between July and November 1973. One example, No D8568, is preserved in working order at faraway Chinnor in Oxfordshire, following a spell in industrial use. *Derek Cross*

Far left: Train 1E83 again — the 14.15 Edinburgh–Newcastle semi-fast — this time departing from Edinburgh Waverley behind 'Deltic' No 9015 *Tulyar*. The mixed rake of stock and the vans confirm the secondary status of this train, even though it retained its Class 1 reporting number. The 124-mile journey to Newcastle would take three hours, with three stops in Scotland alone at Prestonpans, Longniddry and Dunbar.

No 9015 was new from Vulcan Foundry in late 1961, being first allocated to Finsbury Park in North London. She remained in BR service until January 1981, when withdrawn from York. Preserved by the Deltic Preservation Society, *Tulyar* has now spent longer under DPS control than with British Rail. *Tulyar* was the name of the horse that won the 1952 Derby. Successful racehorses and British regiments were the two themes for the 22 'Deltic' names. Six of the production 'Deltics' survive in preservation. *Derek Cross*

Above: No 1971 in 1971! Brush Type 4 No 1971 is pictured about to depart from Edinburgh Waverley in April 1971 with an Aberdeen to London express. In those days this train, the 10.30 Aberdeen–King's Cross direct service, took 10 hours, with a scheduled arrival at King's Cross after 10 stops at 20.30. The HSTs that replaced the locomotive-hauled trains more than 20 years ago can do the same journey in just over seven hours. Their 125mph top speed, increased horsepower of two power cars and much greater acceleration make a great deal of difference.

No 1971 was only six years old when photographed, having been introduced new to Haymarket depot in Edinburgh in October 1965. Renumbered to 47270 in March 1974, the locomotive has performed a further 30 years' service, latterly as a Freightliner locomotive named *Cory Brothers* mainly hauling intermodal container trains to and from the deep-sea ports in England. *Derek Cross*

Left: Dalry Junction in north Ayrshire was a favourite Derek Cross photographic location — close to his home, a friendly accessible signalbox with, like him, a pipe-smoking signalman, lots of variety, both freight and passenger, a range of semaphore signals and some very nice views in the late afternoon if the sun was out.

Pictured on 23 July 1973, English Electric Type 3 No D6904 is setting off from the loop with a Cadder to Ardrossan oil special. Following a diesel unit to Stranraer via Ayr, the freight would get as far as Kilwinning, three and a half miles distant, before branching off onto the branch to Ardrossan and Largs.

Although the Class 37s became common in Scotland later (some remain allocated to Motherwell depot for West Highland work even today), they were not very common back in 1973. No D6904 became 37204 then 37378, and was scrapped by Booths in Rotherham in 1996. *Derek Cross*

Below left: This August 1976 view sees Class 40 No 40158 accelerating away from the Kilmarnock stop on 1S49, the daily Leeds to Glasgow Central service. A Class 40 on this train was very rare. The London St Pancras–Glasgow Central service, the 'Thames–Clyde Express', and 1S49 were for many years the preserve of 'Peak' diesels of Classes 45 and 46. The substitute Class 40 would seem to suggest a failure of the booked locomotive. The rigours of the Settle & Carlisle and Glasgow & South Western perhaps proved too much for the 'Peaks', although they were generally reliable machines. Later on 1Co-Co1 diesels were banned from Glasgow Central owing to a number of derailments, although I think the through Leeds and Sheffield services to Glasgow had stopped by the time the ban was introduced.

Kilmarnock was a large and important regional station with six platforms at one time, with the bay platforms seen here on the right being used for local commuter services to Glasgow via Barrhead and to the Ayrshire coast. *Derek Cross*

The signals and signalbox in the background tell us that the Glasgow–Stranraer service has just passed Lochgreen Junction, south of Troon, in Ayrshire. The train will have started at Glasgow Central and, having stopped at Troon, will go forward to Prestwick, Ayr and all stations to Stranraer. The distance from Glasgow to Stranraer Harbour is a surprising 101 miles.

The purpose of the junction at Lochgreen was to allow the Troon avoiding line to go off to the right, and was also the access to the then railway wagon repair shops at Barassie, sadly all now closed.

Nine-car formations were not common and referred to locally as 'triples'. Sometimes trains would divide at Ayr with only the front unit or units going forward to the Irish Sea ferry port.

As many of you will recognise, the train is in the midst of the Open Championship Golf Course, Royal Troon, with the clubhouse on the left above the cab of the unit. The picture was taken on 28 May 1975. *Derek Cross*

Below: After sitting in Ayr station, idling before its return trip to Glasgow Central, a Swindon-built Class 126 DMU is seen setting off for Glasgow on the morning of 9 April 1970. Typically, the initial movement of these Class 126 DMU sets was accompanied by clouds of blue smoke, evident here drifting over the Kyle Street sidings.

These three-car units spent almost all their working lives on the non-electrified lines of the Clyde coast south of Glasgow. They were based at Corkerhill depot, in Glasgow, and they had an extension to the old steam shed built for them in Ayr in the early 1960s. In an era where disused railway buildings litter the country, it is pleasing to report that Ayr depot is still in use today as a wagon repair facility for the local coal wagons used across the Ayrshire coalfield and sea terminal at Hunterston. *Derek Cross*

Right: On a day trip to Ayr on 27 July 1973, English Electric Class 40 No 379 creeps across the bridge over the River Ayr into Ayr station. The day trip had originated in Nelson in Lancashire and the Class 40, recently ex-works by its appearance, had in all likelihood brought the train, 1Z97, all the way.

Ayr, on the coast, with its kind climate, long sandy beach and the lure of Burns' country, was a common destination for day trips (these were called 'Adex' — 'Advertised Day Excursions') or Merrymaker excursions from stations in the north of England or even the east coast of Scotland. When the day excursions were not in the timetable, there were often specials to Ayr races, the only Grade One racecourse in Scotland. In earlier years the specials had also served the Butlin's camp at Heads of Ayr. These excursion services were common in steam days and continued into the diesel era; sadly now in the electric era they are very rare.

No 40179 had a working life of just 19 years, from 1962 to 1981, being withdrawn from Wigan Springs Branch in February that year. *Derek Cross*

55

Waiting to leave Ayr station with a school special to Largs is Class 25 No 25011. The date is 2 June 1978 and the local education authority was still using rail transport to get school children to Largs for a boat trip to Millport on the nearby island of Great Cumbrae. A morning departure from Ayr to Largs would see the return arrive back in Ayr at around five o'clock.

In the background a Class 126 DMU lurks in Kyle Street sidings, by this date in blue and grey livery. No 25011, the former D5161, was one of the early

Class 25s. Built at Darlington, the locomotive was new to the nearby shed at Thornaby (51L) in September 1961. In traffic for less than 20 years, the locomotive was withdrawn from Haymarket at the end of 1980 and cut up at BREL Swindon in March 1981.

Although the DMU sidings are now built upon, the station and the hotel remain unchanged today save for modern catenary. *Derek Cross*

Steam had been gone from the Ayrshire coalfield for five years (3/10/66) and the Class 20s and 25s had taken over. Unusually, No 8104 is working solo as it passes through the closed station at Drongan on 1 December 1971, in the typical low light of the Scottish winter.

At that time Drongan was a junction and still had an operating signalbox, as the semaphore in the background confirms. The train is a rake of empty coal wagons (a mix of MCOs and MCVs) from Falkland Junction to Littlemill colliery. Once at the colliery, the empties would be swapped for loaded wagons before the trip returned back to Ayr Harbour. Much of the coal from the Ayrshire

coalfield at that time was exported to Northern Ireland from the railway, owned British Transport Docks Board (BTDB) port at Ayr.

Class 20s, as these locomotives became, normally worked in pairs because, as well as giving more horsepower, the train crew had much better visibility driving from a cab at each end of the pair of locomotives.

As No D8104 the locomotive had been new to Glasgow Eastfield exactly 10 years earlier in December 1961. The locomotive was built for English Electric by Robert Stephenson & Hawthorn in Darlington and remained a Scottish Region locomotive for much of its working life. *Derek Cross*

Below: The late 1970s saw the first change from corporate Rail Blue for almost 15 years. In 1978 a white livery for DMUs was announced and trialled. Pictured here near Waterside on the freight-only Dalmellington branch is the 'white DMU' on a Branch Line Society (BLS) excursion in September 1978. The special train was on a tour of the freight-only branches in Ayrshire that day and appears to be well loaded.

On the right of the train are tell-tale signs of the immense amount of mining that went on in this area. First iron ore and later coal were extracted from these hills around Dalmellington, and indeed modern diesels still trundle along this branch line collecting open cast coal from the surrounding area. Recently opened in Waterside is the Dunaskin Heritage Centre, which commemorates the area's rich industrial past and includes a preserved railway line and railway museum. *Derek Cross*

Right: Hurrying southwards across the River Annan is Brush Type 4 No D1956. The train is the 1M69 Perth–Kensington Olympia Motorail service, comprising coaches and, at the rear of the train, bogie car flats with private motor cars on board. Popular at that time to avoid congested roads, the Motorail concept was sadly one that did not catch on. Perhaps it could still have an Anglo-Scottish role, as the concept works well on the Continent.

Annan was then the last Scottish station on this line, being just 17 miles north of Carlisle and therefore only 8 miles from the border at Gretna, where the River Sark divides the two countries.

No D1956, then a 'Western lines' machine, was common on the WCML in the early 1970s and went on to become No 47260 in 1974, 47553 later in 1974 and finally 47803 in 1989. The photograph was taken in September 1971. *Derek Cross*

An obviously ex-works Brush Type 4 No D1689 accelerates away from the stop at Dumfries with a London, Euston to Glasgow relief on 17 July 1971. With just 82 miles to go before reaching Glasgow, the train would stop once more at Kilmarnock. Train 1S58 was a relief service to the 1S57 'Royal Scot'.

Dumfries had been a major junction with branches to Lockerbie and the 'Port Road' to Stranraer via Newton Stewart, as well as being a principal station on the Nith Valley line. By 1971, however, the branches had closed and only the main line remained. Today, the station remains well kept and has services direct to Glasgow, Stranraer, Carlisle and Newcastle.

No D1689 was originally a Western Region locomotive. Converted to electric train heating and given the new identity of 47486 in February 1974, the locomotive only lasted in traffic until mid-1987, being condemned and scrapped at Berry's in Leicester later that year. *Derek Cross*

The arrival of a long troop special from Warcop, near Appleby, to Stranraer Harbour has led to a flurry of shunting at the harbour station on 27 May 1978. Sulzer No 25056 has released the train engine, English Electric Class 40 No 40107, and is pushing the empty stock back into the station platform for the return trip. It is likely the train was involved in moving troops to and from Northern Ireland. The normal services to this major ferry port on the southwest coast of Scotland were DMUs to Glasgow and the 'Paddy', the night train to and from London Euston. All these services connected with the regular ferry service to Larne in Northern Ireland.

Class 40s and 25s were common in Ayrshire in the 1970s but what is less usual is that both of these locomotives were at the time allocated to Longsight depot in Manchester, over 200 miles away. *Derek Cross*

Crossing the River Nith just north of Dumfries on the former GSWR Nith Valley line is Class 47 No D1842 at the head of a Glasgow to London relief. This river crossing is known as Portrack Viaduct — today, ironically, the viaduct has not survived but the locomotive has! The bridge in the photograph, which had been built in the late 19th century, has recently been replaced by a modern, essentially concrete structure.

At this time between 1971 and 1973 the Nith Valley line was used as a diversionary route, as in this photograph, whilst the main line over Beattock was upgraded and electrified. Today the Nith Valley's role is reversed, a large number of freight trains now using the route in order to keep the electrified line over Beattock clear for fast passenger trains.

No D1842, which became No 47192, was withdrawn 18 years ago in 1987 although some Class 47s remain in traffic today in 2005! Now preserved on the Churnet Valley Railway at Cheddleton, near Stoke on Trent, the locomotive should be back in service later in 2005 after an overhaul. *Derek Cross*

In the days before cheap air travel and holidays abroad became commonplace, a large number of Scottish people would traditionally holiday on the Lancashire coast in July. The resorts of Morecambe, Fleetwood and the more popular Blackpool all attracted a large number of specials every summer. The Glasgow Fair fortnight would see several excursions go south and the exercise would be repeated northbound a fortnight later.

Pictured at Closeburn, 12 miles north of Dumfries in glorious evening light on 11 August 1973, English Electric Class 40 No 208 is speeding south with an empty stock working from Paisley to Manchester Red Bank carriage sidings, train reporting number 5Z38. Earlier in the day the locomotive and stock had worked the return holiday excursion from Blackpool to Paisley as train 1Z38. As No D208, one of the first batch of English Electric Type 4s, this locomotive had been allocated new to Finsbury Park back in August 1958. Later cascaded to the LM/Scottish Regions, the locomotive was withdrawn in 1982 from Longsight depot in Manchester.
Derek Cross

Below: With a train of prefabricated track, Class 20 No D8080 passes south of Closeburn on 9 September 1971. The train is a special, travelling from the CCE depot in Irvine to the wayside station of Racks, some four miles south of Dumfries, in preparation for some weekend relaying. Irvine at that time was a large engineering depot, which serviced much of southern Scotland. As Irvine had no locomotive depot, the locomotives for trains generally came from the depot in Ayr.

No D8080 was built in Darlington for English Electric and delivered straight to Scotland back in August 1961, to Eastfield depot (then 65A). Much of the locomotive's working life was spent in Scotland and it was withdrawn from service in July 1990.

The Class 20s performed all sorts of tasks in Scotland for many years and, indeed, DRS machines can still be seen at work in Scotland nearly 50 years after being introduced; in addition there are more than 30 in preservation. They have been the real success of the small early modernisation diesels. *Derek Cross*

Right: On a Saturday evening in August 1973 we are at Closeburn again, three miles south of Thornhill on the Glasgow–Dumfries line, to see 5Z40, a long empty stock train heading south from Glasgow to Manchester.

Earlier in the day the train would have conveyed returning Scottish holidaymakers home and was now running as a Class 5 empty coaching stock, or 'ECS', as these trains were commonly known.

The train is hauled by two Class 25s, Nos 7639 and 7669. Although the locomotives are identical, and separated by only 30 running numbers, they were built by different companies, No 7639 by Beyer Peacock in 1965 (delivery new to Sheffield Darnall) and 7669 by BR at Derby much later in March 1967, when it was delivered to DO1, the London Division of the LMR. They were both broken up at Swindon within a year of each other in 1985. *Derek Cross*

Left: Elsewhere in the book we see an excursion from Nelson to Ayr in 1973; some three years earlier, on 21 August 1970, we see another. This time the train is an outward day excursion from Barrow-in-Furness to Ayr, pictured crossing over the viaduct at Carronbridge, two miles north of Thornhill and just before the famous Drumlanrig Tunnel and gorge. The train has just over 40 miles to go and the weather that day in southern Scotland is looking fine.

Regrettably, the named locomotive No 211 *Mauretania* appears to have lost its nameplate. We can clearly see where the nameplate, with a crest, should have been!

Frustratingly, on the Nith Valley Line today the unchecked growth of vegetation alongside the railway lines has led to pictures, such as this one and of the beautiful Ballochmyle Viaduct near Mauchline, being virtually unobtainable. Although these excursions to Ayr have ceased there is a multitude of freight traffic on this line that would still look well on some of these old Glasgow & South Western Railway structures. *Derek Cross*

Above: This August 1973 picture is of 'Peak' No D137 approaching Sanquhar, some 56 miles south of Glasgow on the ex-GSWR Nith Valley route. The train is 1E49, the Saturdays-only Glasgow–Leeds (not 1E59 as shown), which, having stopped at Kilmarnock, and at Kirkconnel, will then go on to Dumfries, Annan and Carlisle, before heading over the Settle & Carlisle line to Leeds.

No D137, named *The Cheshire Regiment* in June 1966, was the last Class 45 to be built, entering service in December 1961 at Derby. Six months after this photograph was taken it was renumbered 45014 and remained in traffic until March 1986. Withdrawn as a result of a collision at Chinley on 10 March 1986, the locomotive was scrapped in Manchester later that year. *Derek Cross*

Left: Coming off the Edinburgh line at Strawfrank Junction, immediately south of Carstairs station, onto the West Coast main line is Brush Type 4 No 1696 on 25 April 1970. The train is a Bathgate to Kings Norton (Birmingham) car train, surprisingly with the correct reporting number, 4M45.

After joining the WCML, the route to Kings Norton is straightforward through Carlisle and Crewe and on to the West Midlands. No D1696 was new to Derby shed in December 1963 and later became 47108. In the background some Class 20s wait in the loop to follow the train to Beattock. *Derek Cross*

Below: As well as being a busy triangular junction station, Carstairs was surrounded by a number of small goods yards. Pictured here from the overbridge at the station is the yard immediately to the east, with the locomotive depot on the far right. The contents of this yard back in the spring of 1973 appear to be engineering-related, with an early track machine also visible.

Setting off from the yard, which is still semaphore-signalled, is Haymarket-allocated No 5150, the final Class 24 built, with an engineer's train heading north towards Lanark Junction. Less than a year later in April 1974 No 5150 would become 24150. New to Gateshead in January 1961, the locomotive remained in traffic until December 1976. *Derek Cross*

Left: No book on Scottish diesels would be complete without pictures in the snow! I am sure there was more snow in Scotland in the 1970s than there is today but there was also less high-speed (ISO) film to help with recording these scenes. Good snow shots are difficult — how many of you have, like me, taken pictures in the snow that appear too dark?

This one, however, taken on the morning of 4 January 1976 at Carstairs, has come out not too badly. It shows three different classes of locomotive either moving very slowly or stopped — the secret of a half-decent picture! Arriving from Edinburgh is English Electric Class 40 No 40061 on a relief Edinburgh to Birmingham service, 1M60. Once stopped, an electric locomotive would hook onto the other end of the train and set off down the Clyde Valley, where the weather probably deteriorated as it made its way through the Southern Uplands — Beattock Summit is 1,015ft above sea level.

Also in the picture on the former Carstairs shed (ex-66E), a stabling point in 1976, can be seen from left to right, Class 24 No 24128 and Class 26 No 26020. *David Cross*

Above: In 1970 most major stations had a goods yard where often you would find a locomotive pottering about engaged in endless shunting operations, moving a wagon here, another there, often for no obvious purpose!

On a sunny August afternoon in 1970 we see BRCW Type 2 No 5325 engaged in just such duties in one of the small yards adjacent to the northbound platform at Carstairs Junction. Also of note are the semaphore signals, the signal gantry on the south side and the imposing Caledonian Railway signalbox.

The locomotive, new as No D5325 from BRCW at Smethwick to Haymarket shed in Edinburgh in May 1959, worked its entire career north of the border.

Unusually for the early 1970s, there is a lot of litter about in the yard and I don't mean the green DMU car in the yard and steam engine tenders in the distance! *Derek Cross*

No book on diesels in Scotland would be complete without, arguably, the high spot of diesel traction in Scotland — pairs of Class 50s on the West Coast expresses, 5,400hp of English Electric muscle!

Before its later fame, we see Class 50 No D407 in multiple with companion No D436, hard at work on the West Coast main line, when no more than three years old. Subsequently, No D407 went on to be named first *Hercules* (from April 1978 to February 1984) and later *Sir Edward Elgar*, complete with special green livery, and is today preserved in this livery at the Midland Railway Centre in Butterley, Derbyshire. No D436, later named *Victorious*, was less lucky, being scrapped at Rotherham in the early 1990s.

Back on 15 August 1970, Nos D407 and D436 were photographed passing Lamington, some 11 miles south of Carstairs, on the northbound 'Royal Scot', 1S57, from Euston to Glasgow. The train would have been electrically hauled from Euston to Crewe, where a pair of Class 50s would have taken over for the journey to Glasgow. This was an interim arrangement before full electrification to Glasgow was introduced in 1974 under the 'Electric Scots' banner. Once electrification arrived, the Class 50s were transferred to the Western Region, working from London to Bristol, Exeter and Plymouth until the early 1990s. *Derek Cross*

On 24 March 1970 the southbound 'Royal Scot' (1M20) heads through the Clyde Valley with a single Class 50, No D416. The 'Royal Scot' at that time was scheduled for a single locomotive but six weeks later, from 4 May 1970, pairs of Class 50s started work to give Glasgow to Euston timings of just six hours. The inset shows the commemorative ashtray issued in connection with this service improvement — how marketing has changed over the years! The little signalbox at the closed wayside station is still open and would continue to operate until all manual boxes in the Clyde Valley were replaced by the Motherwell power signalbox when electrification came some four years later.

No D416 worked on the WCML from new in 1968 until 1974, when transferred away to Plymouth Laira. On the Western Region the locomotive was named *Barham* and lasted in traffic until 1990. Later dismantled at the former Eastern Region works at Stratford in East London, it had had connections with all BR regions. *Derek Cross*

Left: A particular favourite location for Derek Cross was the viaduct over the infant River Clyde near Crawford in southern Lanarkshire, some 47 miles from Glasgow. The location was best for northbound trains during the afternoon, especially if the sun was out — by no means a certainty in the Southern Uplands of Scotland.

Nevertheless, 11 August 1973 was just such a day when it all came together for Derek to capture Brush Type 4 No D1694, heading north over the bridge with train 1S46, the mid-morning Manchester Victoria–Glasgow express. No D1694 had been new to Old Oak Common in December 1963. After 25 years in traffic the locomotive was withdrawn from Sheffield Tinsley (as 47106) in early 1988 and was cut up at the Berry yard in Leicester in June 1989.
Derek Cross

Above: In the spring of 1970 — in post-steam but pre-electric days — the 10-mile slog up Beattock Bank northbound still required banking engines.

The shed at Beattock in the diesel era was just a shed, without fuel or facilities. That meant that each week the three Class 20s had to be changed and this usually took place on a Saturday. The exchange came from Polmadie or perhaps Motherwell depot, and here we see the three 'new' bankers travelling south through Carstairs to Beattock on 25 April 1970. The locomotives are Nos D8110 (since preserved), D8057 and D8125, two in blue, one in green, two bonnet-first, the other cab first. Dominating the scene is the spectacular signal gantry at the north end of Carstairs station. A 100-mile round trip light engine movement was perhaps not very efficient, but it did make for some interesting photographic opportunities of Class 20s on the West Coast main line in Scotland.
Derek Cross

Left: Just about there! A southbound Aberdeen–London express (1M61) has the summit in sight as the train approaches Beattock Summit from the north. Another 500 yards will see the train begin the 10-mile descent to Beattock station and on through Lockerbie to Carlisle.

This picture, taken on 1 August 1970, captures the changeover from steam days to the modern railway — a two-year-old hi-tech English Electric 2,700hp diesel, maroon Mk 1 carriages and semaphores, all in the bleakness of rural Dumfriesshire.

The Class 50 locomotives left LMR/SCR during the mid-1970s for the Western Region, No D420, built at Vulcan Foundry in Newton-le-Willows in May 1968, leaving in 1974. Subsequently named *Revenge* in February of that year, the locomotive lasted in traffic until July 1990, when it was withdrawn from Laira depot in Plymouth, being scrapped at Booth's in Rotherham in 1991. *Derek Cross*

Left: I clearly remember this day, Wednesday 29 March 1970 (we missed my sister's birthday!), when Derek and I sneaked off to the Clyde Valley. The Perth–Manchester Red Bank empty van train was always an interesting working with unpredictable motive power.

BRCW/Sulzer Type 2 No 5330 had been given the task of hauling the long train of empty parcel/newspaper vans back to Manchester. As the southbound WCML approaches the signalbox at Beattock Summit, the line curves to the right before emerging from under a farm bridge at the end of the loop. That day we heard the 1,160hp of the locomotive, with its peculiar noise that Derek always thought sounded like an agricultural chaff-cutter, before we saw the train struggle over the summit and on towards Carlisle. There the Type 2 would normally give way to a Type 4 to take the vans through to Manchester. *Derek Cross*

Pictured on the descent of the 10-mile Beattock Bank at Harthope we see Class 50s Nos 413 and 449 on 1M35, the 13.10 Glasgow Central to Euston service in the early summer of 1973.

This whole landscape has now changed with the new M74 no longer continuing under the railway line but rather cutting across the hill behind the train. Within three years the locomotives had moved on, No 413 to Plymouth Laira and No 449 to Bristol, electric traction having taken over the Anglo-Scottish services in 1974. The locomotives later carried the names *Agincourt* and *Defiance* respectively, and the latter locomotive is still with us, preserved on the Severn Valley Railway. *Derek Cross*

Above: The village of Ecclefechan in Dumfriesshire is probably more famous as being the birthplace of Thomas Carlyle, the writer, who was born there in 1795 before moving to nearby Annan Academy to study.

Some 176 years later the small Caledonian signalbox was of more interest to Derek Cross. Although the station had been closed to passengers on 13 June 1960, the signalbox and crossing remained in use when this picture was taken in July 1971.

A Saturdays-only summer dated train has been called into the old platform to receive some instructions from the signalman, seen walking across the track to speak to the second man on the Class 37.

On summer Saturdays all available motive power was pressed into service, as the use of No D6853 confirms. The train is a Blackpool–Glasgow service, which would normally have been hauled by either a Type 4 locomotive or a pair of Type 2 Class 25s.

No D6853 was by this time allocated to Glasgow Eastfield, having started life at Landore in Swansea. Interestingly, the research for this book highlighted that No D6853 was not alone in this regard, with over 150 of the entire class of '37s' being first allocated to sheds in South Wales. *Derek Cross*

Back cover: The eastern end of Platform 1 at Edinburgh Waverley has long been a focus for photographers and enthusiasts alike. Very little has changed there in over 30 years, except motive power.

On 11 March 1972 we see green Brush Type 4 No D1764 waiting to head an express south to London King's Cross, being passed by 'Deltic' *Tulyar.* I am not sure what the correctly uniformed second man complete with British Rail hat finds so amusing — perhaps the fact that anyone would want to photograph a grimy seven-year-old Class 47!

Although a pretty nondescript locomotive in 1972, No D1764 went on to be a minor celebrity as No 47581 *Great Eastern*, the pride of Stratford depot in East London when services on the line to Norwich were Class 47-hauled.

Both locomotives survived until very recently. *Tulyar* is preserved at Barrow Hill in Derbyshire and No D1764, latterly numbered 47763, was only recently scrapped by private contractors at Motherwell depot. *Derek Cross*